WHEN THE CHILD
FELL ILL

WHEN THE CHILD FELL ILL

A PLAY BY CHARLOTTE S. AKYEAMPONG

© Copyright 2018 by Charlotte S. Akyeampong

All Rights Reserved. Without limiting the rights under the copyright reserved above, this book may not be reproduced, in whole or in part, stored in a retrieval system, or transmitted in any form or by any means (electronic, mechanical, photocopying, recording, or otherwise) except for brief quotations in critical reviews or publications without the prior permission of the publisher or author.

Library of Congress Cataloging-in-Publication Data

When the Child Fell Ill, by Akyeampong, Charlotte S.

ISBN: 978-1-7323519-8-1

Includes bibliographical references and index
1. Literature   2. Performing Arts   3. General   I. Title

Editor: E. Obeng-Amoako Edmonds

First Edition

Rights for publishing this work or in non-English languages are administered by Ink City Press, in partnership with Atlantic BG Media.

TABLE OF CONTENTS

Introduction... XIII
Synopsis/Characters... XV

Act I   Scene I – Draped in Gloom................. 1
               Scene II – Darkness Deepens............. 17

Act II   Scene I - Unexpected Twist................ 35
               Scene II – Withered Hope.................. 67

Act III   Scene I – Cheering Ray...................... 79
               Scene II – Sweet Sounds.................... 93
               Scene III – Brightest and Best........ 109

Afterword.. 135
Cast/Crew 137

DEDICATION

To my parents, Robert and Betsey Newton, and my big sister, Adelaide, who sowed in me the love for reading and writing at a very tender age.

To my husband, Professor Daniel Afedzi Akyeampong—a mathematician, theoretical physicist, lover of literature, avid reader and renowned scholar—words will not aptly describe the joy of a life you made possible for me to experience. You read every play over and again, and irrespective of how many times you saw the performances on stage—and you saw every single one—the pride and cheer in your smile never faded. It gave me the confidence to dream aloud.

To my children Angelo, Adrian and Adeline for their remarkable support. To my grandchildren, whom I am so proud of, for their love.

To my friends, siblings, nieces and nephews, and all well-wishers for their encouragement. To the cast and crew for touching many hearts with their excellent performances of the play.

To my numerous other children, especially my cherished old students of Presec-Legon (Odadeεs) for their loving kindness, and for their positive contributions to their society.

To Obeng-Amoako Edmonds for his magnanimity in making it possible for this play to be published.

To God Almighty be all glory and praise for the things He has done in my life.

INTRODUCTION

A young child's health hangs in the balance, and the reality that unfolds around him becomes a portrait of some of the complex natures of humankind and the virtues or other factors that instruct our choices.

The setting is a Ghanaian town, but the truth of the plot may very well replay in any village, town or city anywhere in the world. As if they were struck by a blinding light at night, a family is left alone when they need a father the most. The betrayal is painful and the family, left with little money and a sick child to care for, find themselves gasping for air. Life, seen through the predicament of the sick child, affirms a faith that God indeed works everything out in the end.

"When the Child Fell Ill" turns out to be a bold attempt at addressing some of the cultural concerns and expectations in society: childbearing, childlessness, infant mortality, the role of a man in society, and the influence of extended family on marriage. The lead characters, Kenny, Ayeh and Dola are three men who struggled to make ends meet, scrounging for odd jobs, and are willing to risk their own lives for the opportunity of a lifetime. They walk through an open door, unsure of what awaits them, but quickly convince themselves of an adage that becomes the driving force of their lives: nothing ventured, nothing gained.

"When the Child Fell Ill" is an intriguing blend of prose, poetry and song. There are moments that are piercingly sad, and others where the reader and audience can find solace in hope. In every scene, we find in the characters some of the simple, yet poignant attitudes that define our choices both small and great, and all of which are carefully woven into the tapestry of our lives and those of our families.

The scenes are carefully and truthfully punctuated by songs that aptly complement the dialogue. The plot seems to propose that, where the unfortunate sides of a society's culture and individual convictions collide, what is often left behind are traces of regret, mistrust and pain. The only truthful spectator is God, who can bring joy at the unsuspected moments of our lives.

Charlotte Akyeampong's "When the Child Fell Ill" leaves behind a lasting and truly captivating afterglow and lessons worth carrying along through life.

SYNOPSIS

Amy is married to Teddy. The two have already lost two of their three children. So when Nyamekye, their only surviving child suddenly falls ill, it triggers all kinds of reactions from various angles.

CHARACTERS:

MAA BEA	– A respectable middle-aged widow
AMY	– Maa Bea's daughter
LAILA	– Amy's friend
YABA	– Amy's friend
AWO	– Yaba's mother/Maa Bea's friend
AYA	– Laila's mother/Maa Bea's friend
NYAMEKYE	– Amy's sick child
KENNY	– A young entrepreneur
DOLA	– A young entrepreneur
AYEH	– A young entrepreneur
TEDDY	– Amy's husband/Nyamekye's father
AFI	– Teddy's mother
1ST ELDER	– Afi's family member
2ND ELDER	– Afi's family member
NIKKI	– Nyamekye's friend
AKU	– Nikki's mother
MAN	
DANCERS	

ACT I, SCENE 1

DRAPED IN GLOOM

(Living room of MAA BEA. Her daughter AMY is inside with her sick child NYAMEKYE. MAA BEA is busy preparing the child's meal. AMY comes out holding a small wet towel.)

AMY
Mother, the temperature is refusing to go down. This is the third sponging in such a short time, and he is still burning hot like the sun itself. I'm afraid mother, very much afraid.

MAA BEA
Don't be afraid, my daughter. Nyamekye is not going to die. He will be alright. God is in control. You need some rest yourself. Come, sit down, and let me take over. I've just finished his meal and I'll go in and feed him.

AMY
You mean you have prepared fresh meal again for Nyamekye? Oh mother, how can I thank you?

MAA BEA

You don't have to thank me, my child. Of what use is my life if I don't help you in times like these? Let's hope he eats the food. That's all that matters.

(MAA BEA goes in.)

AMY

Throwing away food after food because his meal must always be fresh; sponging him every now and then to beat down the ever rising temperature, buying drugs upon drugs till every money on us is gone. And yet he gets no better.

(Enter MAA BEA.)

AMY

Any luck? Did he eat the food? Talk to me, Mother. Did he eat the food?

MAA BEA

No, Amy, he did not. Much as I tried he did not sip even a teaspoonful, neither did he open his eyes to see who was with him. But we will not give up! God is in control.

AMY

Oh, when will all this be over? Is he also going the way of his brother and sister? I thought I had done with child burying. The two after you, Nyamekye, have decided to go back where they came from, leaving you alone with me. You are now a great source of comfort to us. Like any other child you run and play around, filling our home with laughter and love. You have enjoyed good health these eight years of your life. Why then is this sudden fit of fever which does not want to leave you free? Oh God, why? Why should I be denied a mother's pleasure of holding and cherishing the fruits of her womb? Will my sorrow know no end? Will my tears forever flow? Father, please don't let him die...

          MAA BEA *(placing her arms around AMY)*
No, he will not die. Don't feel this way Amy, God is in control.
          (AMY begins to cry as she sings.)

          AMY
Father, please don't let him die!
Spare my son, my only child.
He is my hope, my life and my all.
Save him, Lord, save him for me!
          (MAA BEA joins in.)

Take him in your loving arms,
And make him healthy once more.
Wipe away our fears and tears,
Spare him, Lord, spare him his life.

          MAA BEA
Stop crying my child, you do yourself no good. Nyamekye is ill, yes, very ill, but that does not mean he can't recover. Have faith in God, my child, give him time. He will get better. The medicine he is taking will work. All these drugs will not be in vain.

AMY

The drugs, how long are we going to buy these drugs, the prices of which keep going up? The drugs are too expensive, mother, and they are consuming all your money. Very soon we shall have no money left to buy anything at all in this house. Don't think I haven't seen you selling some of your valuables on the quiet, just to support us. All these precious things that meant so much to you and Papa...

MAA BEA

Don't worry Amy; your dear father, if he were alive, would have readily approved of my disposing of them to save a life, especially that of his own grandchild. After all, what is more precious than life?

AMY

All the same, mother, this can't go on forever. You can't continue selling the family property just like that. Oh, what are we going to do? How are we going to get money to buy the next batch of drugs?

MAA BEA

I say don't worry, Amy. Who knows, Teddy your husband may show up today with something for us.

AMY

Teddy? Since he sent Nyamekye and me over here, has he bothered to show his face to see how we are getting on? Teddy has sent us nothing, not even a word of greeting. He doesn't seem to care anymore. I'm sure he has forgotten we even exist. Perhaps he was eager to get rid of us the day he brought us here. To him, it was "good riddance," but I didn't know then. I trusted him too much to see through his action.

MAA BEA

Amy, my child, you don't know why Teddy has not called. Don't blame anyone unless you have sufficient ground for doing so. For all you know, Teddy is not feeling well himself. It could also be that his official assignment leaves him no time to attend to private matters. His recent promotion has made him a very busy man, and you know that. Besides, he knows you are in capable hands, and that I will do all I can for you and Nyamekye, my grandchild.

AMY

But that is not right. Nyamekye is the responsibility of his parents and not you. We should be looking after you and not the other way round.

MAA BEA

I know you will certainly look after me, when the time comes. Right now it's time for me to help you look after your sick child.
(There is knocking.)

Someone is at the door. It could be Teddy who has come in answer to our prayer. You go in and attend to the child while I receive the visitor.
(AMY goes in. Enter NIKKI, NYAMEKYE'S friend.)

MAA BEA

Oh, it's you, Nikki, coming to see your friend as usual. You do very well, I must say.

NIKKI

How is Nyamekye today? I brought him these flowers. I hope he likes them. Please put them by his bedside. I also brought him the work we did at school and this story book, too. It is very interesting and I know he will love it very much, especially the beautiful pictures in it.

MAA BEA *(receiving the items)*

That's very kind of you Nikki. You are a very good friend.

NIKKI

Can I go in and see him?

MAA BEA

Certainly, my child. Come, let's go in and see your friend. You know he is always happy to see you.
(NIKKI and MAA BEA go in. Enter AKU, NIKKI'S MOTHER, with rage.)

AKU

Nikki, Nikki! This boy is stubborn. I have warned him several times not to come to this house but he doesn't mind me. Come out, Nikki! Nikki, come out, I say!

(Enter NIKKI.)

AKU

Look here, son, haven't I told you never to come to this house? Do you want to die before you obey me? Nyamekye is seriously ill. He is going to die and you will be next if you keep on coming here.

NIKKI

No, mother, don't say that. Nyamekye will not die. He will get well again. I know it. He will get well and the two of us will learn and play together again.

AKU

Oh, shut up there. What do you know about these matters? I tell you this house has become a house of death for children. Two are gone already and your friend is the third to go. After him will be your turn if you don't stop coming here. So listen to me and do as I say, understand? Is he the only friend you have? Don't you have other friends to play with?

NIKKI

But I don't come here to play, mother. I come to keep Nyamekye company and to pray for him. I want him to be well again and I know God will make him well.

(Enter MAA BEA.)

AKU *(her back turned to MAA BEA)*
Oh keep quiet there and listen to me....

MAA BEA

What is the matter? Is something wrong?

AKU *(startled)*

Oh no…er…er, we are going out and I came to fetch Nikki. Come Nikki, hurry up or we shall be late.

MAA BEA

Don't worry, Nikki. Go with your mother. You can visit your friend anytime you are free.

NIKKI *(as he is being dragged away by the MOTHER)*

Sure, I will.

(*Enter AWO and AYA, MAA BEA'S friends who look on with disapproval.*)

AWO and AYA

And why is she dragging the poor child away like that?

MAA BEA

Hmm… do I even know? Some mothers! My sisters, I'm happy to see you here. Not a day passes without your coming over to see us. I'm very grateful to you for your constant support.

AYA

We are only performing our duty, Maa Bea. You would have done the same for us. How can we eat and sleep without knowing what is happening here? We shall come here to support you so long as God gives us strength.

AWO

Yes, Maa Bea. we shall always visit you, to assist and support you in looking after the child. What are friends for if not to make themselves available in times like these? We brought Nyamekye some fruits. By the way, how is he today?

MAA BEA

There is not much improvement, but he is in God's capable hands and we hope for the better.

AYA

Tell me, Maa Bea, is it true that Nyamekye's father has not stepped here since he brought Amy and the child over to you?

MAA BEA

Yes, it is true. He hasn't been here.

AWO *(to AYA)*

You see, I told you.

AYA

And is it true he hasn't sent Amy any message, money or anything that she will need to attend to the child?

MAA BEA

Yes, that is also true. We haven't received anything from Teddy. No word, no money, no visit, no clothing, nothing.

AWO *(to AYA)*
You see it is true, everything is true.

MAA BEA
What is true? You are making me nervous.

AYA
Hmm, Maa Bea, this is for your ears alone, even though it is on all lips in town. We've been hearing it everywhere but didn't know how to tell you.

AWO
Yet, we feel that as friends we should let you know, especially when we found that Teddy has not been coming here.

MAA BEA
What is it? Is Teddy in some trouble? Please don't keep me in suspense.

AWO
Maa Bea, you may not believe it but your son-in-law is moving with another woman!

MAA BEA *(shocked)*
What? Another woman? Teddy?

AWO and AYA
Yes, Teddy!

(Enter AMY, rushing on hearing TEDDY'S name)

AMY
What is it mother, what's wrong with Teddy? I hope he has not come to any harm.

OTHERS
No, no, Amy, Teddy is alright. Go and see to the child.
(AMY goes in, as the others watch to make sure she goes.)

MAA BEA
I don't believe what you are saying.

AWO
It is true, Maa Bea, fear men. Teddy is busy courting another woman. That's why he has no time for Amy and Nyamekye.

AYA
Courting? You put it mildly, Awo. The man is married. Teddy has married another woman and the two are living happily together.

MAA BEA
Teddy married? Impossible! And what do his people say? Are they aware of what he is doing?

AWO
Yes, very much so and they've given him their blessing and support.

AYA

Especially his mother, Afi. That woman has no values. She has literally thrown her weight behind her son, encouraging him all the way.

AWO

I hear she even selected the girl for her son.

AYA

That's Afi for you. I won't put it beyond her. She is capable of anything.

MAA BEA

But this is wrong. Custom does not allow a man like Teddy who is already married, I mean properly married, to abandon his legal wife just like that.

AYA

Maa Bea, you talk as if all people are like you who respect custom and religion and believe in decorum. Your son-in-law and his people do not respect these things. They don't care for propriety.

MAA BEA

No, no, I won't have you speak ill of my in-law. Until I see things with my own eyes, I won't believe a word of what you are telling me. Teddy is a gentleman and will not treat Amy like that. I know he will visit us when he is free.

AWO

All the same, remember that all that glitters is not gold and your son-in-law may not be the perfect gentleman you think he is.

AYA

Yes, Maa Bea, be careful whom you trust. For some men are like snakes that hide under grass and will hiss and spit and bite till you drop dead.

(Enter TEDDY.)

TEDDY

Good day, my mothers..

WOMEN *(surprised)*

Good day, son.

MAA BEA *(excited)*

Welcome, Teddy. We've been expecting to see you here for a long time.

TEDDY

Yes I know. I should have called earlier, but one or two important matters prevented me from doing so.

MAA BEA

I said it. Amy, Teddy is here. Oh you've no idea how glad I am to see you, Teddy. We were very worried when you did not show up and did not send any message. I hope everything is all right with you.

TEDDY

Yes, yes…

(Enter AMY.)

AMY

At long last, Teddy, you are here. We've been expecting you every minute of the hour. How are you? Are you all right?

TEDDY

Yes, I'm fine. Err… you see… I am not alone. I came with my mother and others. They will be here soon.

MAA BEA

Oh, that is great. It's very kind of them to pay us a visit. We are very grateful.
(AWO and AYA look at each other with great surprise and embarrassment and ask permission to leave.)

AWO

Err… Maa Bea, we want to ask permission to leave so that you can have time for your visitors.

AYA

That's right, Maa Bea, do take care of Nyamekye.. We'll call again another time.

MAA BEA and AMY

Thank you and good-bye.

AWO and AYA
Good bye!
(Exit AWO and AYA.)

ACT I, SCENE 2

DARKNESS DEEPENS

(Living room of MAA BEA. Enter AFI and OTHERS accompanied by sound effects)

MAA BEA
Welcome, good people. Please sit down.

AFI
No, we won't sit down. We did not come here to socialise. We shall be leaving soon.

MAA BEA
Amy, bring our visitors some water.

1ST ELDER
No, the water is not necessary. We shall be leaving soon, as she rightly said. My brother, go ahead and tell them why we are here.

2ᴺᴰ ELDER

As you can see, we are very busy people who believe in brevity and precision. We don't have time to waste. Time is precious; time is money so we don't waste time with things that do not matter. Anyway, we did not come all the way here to sit and drink water. We are busy people as I've already said and as such…

AFI *(losing her patience)*

Listen to him, talking of brevity and precision and yet beating about the bush. Just go straight to the point and tell them why we are here or I'll do that myself.

2ᴺᴰ ELDER

Afi, Afi, why are you so impatient? If you can do it yourself, why did you bring me along? In your own wisdom, you found it necessary to invite me here. So keep quiet and let me do the work in my own way.

AFI

It is the time you are wasting that I don't like. Just go straight to the point and tell them why we are here.

2ᴺᴰ ELDER

Who said I am wasting time? I value time. Err…what was I saying before I was rudely interrupted?

AFI

You see? You are doing it again. This is what I call time wasting and I don't like it at all. It drives away my patience.

1ST ELDER

What is wrong with you? You two must learn to comport yourselves in public. What is all this argument for? If you don't mind I will go ahead and tell them our mission here in this house myself.

MAA BEA

Please go ahead and tell us. We are ready to hear you.

1ST ELDER

Maa Bea, our mission is very simple. We are here to dissolve the marriage between our son Teddy and your daughter Amy.

MAA BEA

What! Did I hear you right?

AFI

Yes, you heard him right. Your daughter Amy is no longer the wife of my son Teddy.

AMY

But why? What sin have I committed? And who dissolved our marriage? And when was it dissolved?

MAA BEA

Calm down, my daughter, and let me do the talking. May I please know why my daughter Amy is no longer the wife of your son Teddy, when the two are properly and legally married?

1ST ELDER
Yes, I can tell you that. Teddy has married another woman and does not need this other one here. Amy is therefore no more part of Teddy's life. Simple!

AMY
Teddy married?

MAA BEA
But this is not right. He can't do that!

2ND ELDER
You see, Maa Bea, Teddy is a good man who believes in doing things properly. He is not like other men who have no scruples. That is why he asked us to come here and dissolve and nullify the marital bond between him and Amy properly.

AFI
Let me do the talking now. It's about time you hit the nail hard on the head, not on the sides.

2ND ELDER
Afi, watch your words. Be mindful of how you talk to me.

1ST ELDER
Honestly, you two are disappointing me. Can't you control your tempers?

AFI

Let me do the talking I say. You see, Maa Bea, my son Teddy is a man, a real man and must have strong children to show the world that he is a man. Therefore he needs a proper woman who can give him strong, sturdy, solid sons who can stand the test of time and live to a ripe old age, sons who will keep the family name flourishing and not these weaklings who drop dead before growing their wisdom teeth. Can't you see? Don't you understand? I love my son and I want him to have a normal married life.

1ST ELDER

To tell you the truth Maa Bea, we are not happy at all with the sort of children Amy produces. They are too frail for any man's liking.

2ND ELDER

Besides, they don't live long. One died when he was four years old.

AFI

Four years, seven months and two days, to be precise!

2ND ELDER

And the other one also died when she was only two years old.

AFI

She was exactly two years, two months, three weeks and two days. I have a record of their birth days as well as their death days. Why, Amy, why? What at all do you do to the children you bring into this world?

####### 2ND ELDER
And now this one, Nyamekye, just when we all thought he was going to stay…

####### AFI
Suddenly threatens to go. Oh, this is too much for me *(cries)*. All my grandchildren being sucked away, one by one like lollipops. I won't allow that to continue. I want my grandchildren to live and surround me with happiness in my old age.

####### MAA BEA
But why blame the woman alone for the children born to both of them. Why don't you make both parents responsible for the type of children they bring forth?

####### AFI
Why should I blame my son, Maa Bea? It is your daughter who has a problem. She is abnormal and my grandchildren will be born by a normal healthy woman. Oh, why was I not warned that my son was plunging into deadly waters when he chose Amy as his wife. *(She weeps.)* Teddy deserves a normal life with a normal wife and not this witch of a woman!

####### MAA BEA
Watch your words, Afi!

####### 1ST ELDER
Let me speak, Afi. Stop crying. In short, what we are saying is that there is something about Amy that we don't like, so take

back your daughter, Maa Bea. Stop crying, Afi, you must thank your stars that your son Teddy is still alive. He could have been killed too, you know!

MAA BEA

What are you implying?

AMY

Maa Afi, are you implying that I'm a witch?

AFI

We've stated our case clearly. Draw your own conclusion. All I can say is my son will not marry any abnormal woman whose children don't live long, simple! Oh, my grandchildren! *(She continues to weep.)*

1ˢᵀ ELDER

I say stop crying, Afi, your new daughter-in-law will surely fill your home with healthy, bouncing children.

AMY

What are you saying, me abnormal? A witch? Teddy, why are you quiet? Tell them you will not leave me for another woman. Say you came here because you care for us. Tell them there is nothing wrong with me and you love me.

AFI

Leave him alone, Amy. His mind is made up already.

2ND ELDER
Amy, we have brought all your things so stay where you belong and don't come and worry Teddy again. Give me the schnapps. *(Pouring libation.)* Come, spirits of our forefathers and be our witnesses. From today onwards, Teddy and Amy are no more husband and wife. Their marriage is formally and officially dissolved, cancelled and nullified. Here, Amy get your things and stay with your mother!

(Enter about six people with AMY'S things in a choreographed dance, joined by AFI and the two ELDERS. They put the things down one by one.)

MAA BEA
But this is not right. We don't do things this way. As adults, we have to sit down and discuss the issue and see how best we can help our children get on in life. Marriage is not dissolved easily like this. If you love your son as you claim, why don't you teach him to love and care for his son who is not well, and to support and love his wife who is looking after his son? We should have discussed all that, instead of the drama you just performed here. Don't you think so?

AFI
There is no need for any discussion. When you deal with a case that is shrouded in abnormality, you don't solve it the normal way.

AMY
Aren't you saying anything, Teddy? What do you say to all this strange allegation? Your sick child needs you. Let's go in and see him. Perhaps that will make you stay with us. Your presence may even help him get better.

AFI
No, no, don't bother him Amy, he will not go in. Anybody who sees that thing inside will run away fast. Nyamekye is closer to death than to life. Teddy has suffered too much already, and his mind is now made up. A look at the child will make no difference to him. His mind is already made up!

AMY
Is that what you say too, Teddy? Speak to me, please. Say you care for me and Nyamekye, our son. Let them know you love us, Teddy.

TEDDY
What man will toil hard and be content to reap nothing in return? What man can bear the taunts of his peers as they proudly point to a chain of strong, healthy children as theirs while he has nothing to point to? How long do you want me to suffer this agony and humiliation? Why should I prolong this pain? No Amy, it's over between us. It's all over.

AMY
Was that your voice, Teddy? Was it you who spoke just now?

1ST ELDER
You heard him loud and clear, woman. His mind is firmly made up. Nothing will make him change his mind.

AFI
Well spoken, my son. Not all men are bold to say 'no' to a bad marriage. Well done!

AMY
Teddy, please think of what you are doing. Think of what we mean to each other, the joys and sorrows we've shared together and the help I've been giving you. Your sick child needs your love and support now more than ever. Teddy, please don't leave us. Remember we are your family and we love you dearly.

TEDDY
It's too late, Amy. Nothing will make me change my mind. I go where happiness calls.

MAA BEA
And what is happiness to a man without his wife and child?

TEDDY
I listen to the voice of reason, the voice of my people. A man is a happy man when he has sons to show the world and Nyamekye is not my idea of a son.

MAA BEA. & AMY *(shocked)*
What? How can you say that, Teddy?

AFI
Is that not the truth? Well-spoken my boy, well spoken. There is nothing more to say. You have said it all. Let's leave now.

AMY *(sings)*
Teddy my dear, don't leave me please.
Don't you turn your back on me.

I cannot live my life without you.
For we must both care for our dear sick child.

              TEDDY *(sings)*

You cannot make me change my mind.
You cannot make me change my mind.

             HIS PEOPLE *(sing)*

You cannot make him change his mind.
Oh, no, you cannot make him change his mind

             MAA BEA *(sings)*

Teddy my son, do listen to me.
Life is not a bed of roses.
There are so many ups and downs.
But man must never run from his duties.

             TEDDY *(sings)*

You cannot make me change my mind.
You cannot make me change my mind.

             HIS PEOPLE *(sing)*

You cannot make him change his mind.
You cannot make him change his mind.

             MAA BEA

Think of what you are doing, Teddy.
Your wife and your child need you, today.

Hasty decisions may lead to regret, tomorrow,
So come back to your wife and child, Teddy.

TEDDY *(sings)*
You cannot make me change my mind.
You can not make me change my mind.

HIS PEOPLE *(sing)*
You cannot make him change his mind.
Oh no, you cannot make him change his mind
  (Exit TEDDY and HIS PEOPLE, singing, dancing and teasing.)

AMY
There goes our hope of getting any assistance from Teddy. From now on we are completely on our own, mother.

MAA BEA
God will provide, my daughter. God will surely provide. We are not alone. God is with us.

AMY
How can Teddy do a thing like this, mother? How can he desert us at a time we need him most. Money is no problem to Teddy, and yet here we are struggling to make ends meet. Why is he doing this to us? O God, why? The sight of his own sick child does not even move him. Why, why has Teddy so changed?
  (AMY begins to cry. MAA BEA comforts her.)

MAA BEA

Don't cry, my dear, this is not the end of the world. It is true, Teddy has left you and your father too is dead, but our Heavenly Father lives and because He lives we can face the future.

(Background music: "Because he lives!")
(MAA BEA goes in. AMY crying, sings)

Because he lives, we can face tomorrow.
Because Christ lives, all fear is gone.
And now I know, yes I know
He holds the future,
And life is worth living.
Just because he lives.

(Enter MAA BEA, carrying her purse.)

MAA BEA

Still crying? Cheer up, my child and remember that where there is life, there is hope, and we shall do our best for Nyamekye. Let me see how much I have in my purse.

(She opens it and counts the money inside.)

Well, not much, but at least it can take me to the next town and back.

AMY

Next town? What are you going to do there, mother?

MAA BEA

I still have some valuables I can sell. I couldn't get a good deal here the last time, but I'm sure I'll be lucky in the next town. So cheer up, my daughter. God has a way of solving every problem. Haven't you heard that when He closes one door He opens another? Let me go and get ready.

(MAA BEA goes in.)

AMY

Oh mother, what could I have done without you? You are indeed a gem of a mother, a real friend in times of trouble, a pillar of support and a tower of strength. I thank God for giving me such a wonderful mother.

(Enter MAA BEA.)

MAA BEA

Well Amy, I'm ready to go. I leave you and Nyamekye in God's hands. Take care till I come back.

AMY

Mother, kindly stop at Laila and Yaba's place and tell them to come and keep me company. I can do with their help while you are away.

MAA BEA

Sure, I shall call them for you my child. I know they will be more than delighted to come over and help you. Yaba and Laila are just like their mothers. They have been so good and loyal to you throughout your ordeal. May God bless them! And now Amy, it's good-bye till I come back. But always remember:

(She sings solemnly)

When there is trouble and help far away,
When darkness surrounds you and hope seems to fade,
Leave all to Father God who will take care of you.
Till then keep praying, keep praying my child.
Good-bye Amy, good-bye, till I come back.

AMY

Good-bye mother, good-bye,
May all go well when you're away.
Good-bye till you come back.

(Exit MAA BEA.)
(AMY sits and thinks for some time before speaking.)

AMY

The world is indeed a strange place. Teddy married? I still can't believe it. He brought me here to my mother with all sorts of promises, sweet promises. "You go to your mother's place with the child. I don't want you to be alone when I'm away at work. Your mother will keep you company. I'll come there every day with all the things you need." Lies, all lies and I believed him. Not knowing it was all a way of getting rid of me so that he could marry his so-called strong and normal woman. Well, what can I do? I'm lucky I have my mother with me and I thank God for that. Dear God, give me strength to look after my child.

(She suddenly notices her mother's purse on the chair.)

Oh no! Mother left her purse behind! Mother, Mother! Oh, dear! How do I send it to her? She will need the money for transportation. I must take it to her now. It's urgent. But no, I can't leave Nyamekye alone! What if something happens to him in my absence? Oh, what must I do? Run after mother or stay and look after my child? Yes, that's it. I'll take the purse quickly to mother, leave the door unlocked so that my friends Laila and Yaba can enter when they get here before me. They will surely look after Nyamekye in my absence. Meanwhile, I'll take this bowl of fruits inside, in case Nyamekye wants something to eat. Now, I am off, God take care of my son while I'm away. Mother, here I come with your purse!

(Exit AMY. Music "Because He lives" is played, lights off to signify end of Act I.)

ACT II, SCENE 1

UNEXPECTED TWIST

―――――――――――――

(Same setting as Act I. Enter three men, KENNY, AYEH and DOLA, with their farming tools, feeling very tired and hungry after walking a long distance.)

―――――――――――――

ALL *(offstage, behind the door)*
Hello, is anybody in? Anybody at home?
(They try to open the door which easily opens, to their surprise)

ALL
The door is not locked! How strange!
(They enter cautiously)

ALL *(exploring the house)*
Hello? An empty house? Can't believe this.

KENNY

Well, a roof over our heads at last, after walking endless miles in the scorching sun.

AYEH

And chairs to sit on and rest our weary feet and tired bodies.
(They sit.)

DOLA

But no food to drive away the hunger that is raging in our stomachs.

ALL

Is anybody in? We are three hungry men looking for food. Please come to our aid. Still no response? This is strange. Ah well, we can do with some rest for starters.

KENNY

I must say the draught and the fire have done us a great harm, completely destroying us. Years of hard work gone down the drain, just like that!

DOLA

It was the fire that dealt us the worst blow, coming from nowhere, to wipe away everything we had, at one go, one cruel go, leaving us with nothing but pain to show the world.

AYEH

The farms we struggled to cultivate, the comfortable lodgings we built, our homes, our farms, our machines, our investments, our future all gone, gone…

DOLA
And now look at us, like three beggars roaming the streets day and night, looking for a new place to settle and make a fresh start. To begin life all over again!

KENNY
Life is indeed an endless struggle. We are back to where we took off. No work, no money, no property and nowhere to lay our heads. But thank God we are alive and have our brains and we shall make use of them.

ALL *(sing)*
Oh life can be so unbearable.
This life is harsh. This life is tough.
We've walked and walked and come this far.
We need to live, we must survive.
And so here we are ready to use our brains.

AYEH
What? Still nobody in to help us?

DOLA
Are we to remain here like this, starving till we drop dead or we go back into the street to continue walking on empty stomachs till we collapse and die?

AYEH
Two equally bad options. Which do we prefer, my brothers, to die in here or go out there and die?

KENNY
The first, of course. At least we have shelter and if we are lucky, someone will come to our aid before we drop dead. Anyway, I'm too weak to walk away.

ALL
Oh God, we need food, food, food, we need food!

AYEH
But where at all are the occupants of this house?

DOLA
I don't understand. Why would anybody go out of his house without locking his door?

KENNY
I'll tell you why, so that people like us can enter. We wouldn't be sitting here if the owner had locked up his door.

AYEH
You are right. It may even be an act of God. You see, God has an answer to every problem. Who thought we'll get a room all to ourselves at this time.

KENNY

Besides, this door that has opened for us now may lead to something good later. Perhaps other doors will be opened.

ALL

Amen! So let it be!

DOLA

Until then, God, let the inmates of this house come quickly and give us food, for I am dying of hunger.

AYEH

I can't help wondering who lives here. Is the person rich or poor, kind or ruthless?

KENNY

We can't answer you, Ayeh, but what I can tell you is that whoever lives here is going to be scared to find three men in his room—three miserable-looking strangers!

DOLA

I don't care whether he gets scared of us or not. My worry is whether he will have sufficient food to feed three hungry men. Food is what matters now.

ALL

Oh yes, we need food, food, food. We need food!

KENNY

Then we must have a strategy that will ensure a warm reception for us.

OTHERS

What do you mean?

KENNY

Imagine I am the owner of this house and I come and find you. *(Mimicking owner.)*
Who are you and what are you doing in my house?

OTHERS *(politely)*

Good sir, we are two tired, jobless strangers who are very hungry. Please have pity on us and give us something to eat, and we shall forever be grateful to you.

KENNY

Get out of here, you lazy bones, out of my house! I don't work to feed vagabonds like you. Out, I say!
    (He fiercely chases them away while they scream and plead).

AYEH and DOLA *(panting)*

Oh my goodness, you really scared us, Kenny.
You were just too wicked, Kenny.

KENNY

This is what happens in real life. This is what may happen to us. Pray that the owner does not do worse than that. The world is complex and difficult to understand. Assistance does not readily come to the needy, simply because they look poor and wretched. It is always those who have, who get more of what they already have. Tell me, how often do you see a hungry pauper being invited to a banquet?

AYEH
Never! It is always those who have food in their homes who get invited to such parties.

DOLA
So what do we do? I can't bear the thought of being driven back into the hot merciless street on an empty stomach.

KENNY
The answer is simple. We must be big.

DOLA
Big? How do we do that?

KENNY
We must have respectable professions to boost our image. You know how people look down on our type of profession. But not for long. That perception will soon change, I promise. But until then, let's get respectable jobs.

AYEH
What are you talking about Kenny? How can we get jobs in this room? And not just any job, but respectable ones too?

DOLA
We don't even look presentable after our long walk to attract the so-called respectable jobs.

KENNY
Forget about our looks. We will just play it their way and you will see the difference. Mere mention of a respectable profession will at once make each of us a somebody, and a somebody always stands tall and gets the best of attention wherever he goes.

AYEH
You are right, Kenny. The truth will surely get us the boot, while a lie will fetch us respect and hospitality. Ours is a strange world indeed, where honest men often suffer and are frustrated.

DOLA
Then let us lie quickly and save ourselves from all this suffering. As I said I can't bear to be driven away without food. I'm starving. Hmm, I won't mind being a lawyer—Lawyer Dola.
(They give him cheers as he paces up and down like a lawyer.)

What about you, Ayeh? Be a pilot, a smart pilot. You are cut right for that profession. You will then fly high in the sky over and above all cares and worries.

AYEH *(paces up and down with cheers from his friends)*
Sure, a pilot I will be. Check me out, Pilot Ayeh at your service. But how do I take off with no planes?

DOLA
Create them Ayeh, dream them. That's what we are doing now. We are dreaming beautiful dreams. Feel free and enjoy the moment while it lasts. Oh dear, look!

(Pointing to their tools.)

Pilots and lawyers do not walk about with hoes and cutlasses.

KENNY
You are right, Dola.. We must hide our tools. We should protect our new image or we blow up the strategy. Come tools, I'll hide you under some bushes outside.

(Exit KENNY with the tools.)

AYEH
Oh, hard working and faithful tools, must you also suffer the same degradation as your masters? Must you too go into hiding as your masters now hide their true identity?

DOLA
Don't worry Ayeh, this is only temporary. We shall not hide our true identity for long; neither shall our tools remain hidden for long. We shall certainly pick up the broken pieces of our life, and build our homes and establish our farms again.

(Enter KENNY.)

We shall proudly wield our cutlasses and hoes and raise high our heads, our honour and our reputation, and all people will respect our noble profession more than they've ever done before …

KENNY

Come on, Dola, don't get over excited, don't get carried away.

AYEH

But Kenny, you still haven't picked a profession. Will you be a doctor?

KENNY

Lawyers, doctors, engineers are all fine. But we must play it safe. I think it's better and safer if we all choose the same profession and back one another up. Let's just say we are all teachers.

AYEH

Teachers? Why teachers? And you think being teachers will boost our image?

KENNY

Sure, more than our own profession.

DOLA

But why teachers, Kenny? Teaching is one job I hate most in my life. I can never be a teacher.

KENNY

Neither can you be a lawyer or a doctor or an engineer for that matter.

DOLA

Who says? Don't forget we all did science and chose to major in Agric…

KENNY

Yes, yes, I know. But right now, and for this brief moment that we are in this house, we are only pretending to be teachers for a special reason. That's all.

DOLA

And what will we teach?

KENNY

Nothing!

AYEH and DOLA

Nothing?

KENNY

Yes, nothing. If we happen to get a pupil here in this house, which I doubt very much, we mark whatever exercise he does correct and save ourselves the trouble of explaining things we may not be able to explain.

(They all laugh.)

DOLA and AYEH

The strategy is good. We shall adopt it.

ALL

So, teachers we are, waiting for our host.
This life is harsh, this life is tough.
We've walked and walked and come this far.
We need to live, we must survive,
And so here we are, ready to use our brains.

DOLA

Just imagine, teachers we are.
Teaching what we do not know.
But man must live, so here we are.
To use our heads and use them well.
Or else we flop and face the grill.

AYEH

We must be bold to keep the game.
A harmless trick to pull us through.
No harm is meant, our hearts are clean.
If you're in our shoes you'll do the same.
So give us the cheer and wish us the best.

KENNY

With luck on our side we shall succeed,
And turn our bitter life into a better life.
We deserve a break and we'll get it straight.
As teachers untrained we'll do our best
For those we teach, and take our reward
From Heaven above without delay.

ALL
This life is hard, this life is harsh.
We've walked and walked and come this far.
We need to live, we must survive,
And so here we are, ready to use our brains.

DOLA
I can hear footsteps; quick, let's hide and see who comes in.
(The three men hide. Enter AMY and her friends, LAILA and YABA.)

YABA
Don't fret, Amy, he will be alright.

LAILA
No harm will come to him. God is in control.

AMY
Thanks for coming with me. Please sit down and rest while I go in and check on him
(AMY goes in)

LAILA
Poor Amy, she has gone through so much pain of late. Nyamekye should not die and leave her childless. That will be too much for her to bear. Imagine the stigmatization, the cruel innuendos and insinuations.

YABA
I really admire her spirit. I wonder what I would have done if I were in her shoes. Oh the woes of the childless woman!

(Enter AMY.)

AMY
Thank God, he is asleep just as I left him. Oh how relieved I am. Please come and help me attend to him.

(Girls go in.)
(KENNY, DOLA and AYEH come out from hiding.)

ALL *(excited)*
Gracious Heavens! What a pleasant surprise! Three lovely ladies, three pretty faces!

DOLA
Incredible, I can't believe our luck, three women and no man. Then we shall surely eat and eat well, for women and food are synonymous.

KENNY
Did you notice the gentle look in their eyes, and the beautiful movements of their lips as they spoke? Oh, such lips cannot pronounce any harsh sentence on us.

AYEH
And their voices, did you notice that too? Sweet, silky voices that will melt any man's heart. Oh how lucky we are!

DOLA
Dear God, let them possess kind hearts and plenty of food so that they can feed us generously.

AYEH
I must say, the sight of these pretty ladies has reduced my hunger. I don't feel that hungry any more. Even if they don't have food I won't...

DOLA
Hey, hey, Ayeh, don't bring in that. Remember it was hunger that brought us here, and we are still hungry so we must eat. We need food, all three of us.

AYEH
True, but the open door, as we said earlier, may lead to other things, too. And we must not stand in the way of any good thing that wants to come our way. Shhh... I think they are coming. Quick, let's hide!
(AYEH and DOLA attempt to hide but KENNY pulls them back.)

KENNY
No! No, not this time! For how long do you want to remain hiding? No more hiding! We shall stand here and talk to them.

DOLA and AYEH
What? Are you sure it's the right thing to do? Okay, okay.
(They get ready to face the girls.)

(Enter GIRLS.)

MEN

Good day, ladies!

(GIRLS give a cry of surprise.)

KENNY

Sorry to frighten you.

GIRLS

Who are you?

KENNY

Teachers! We are teachers on our way to a conference... somewhere... next town... to be precise... and we... er... er...

DOLA

We developed some... problems... when we got close to this house... so we... we...

AYEH

So we decided to come in and... ask for... your assistance... Your door was not locked so we entered and we hope... we hope...

DOLA

We hope to pay you back by offering free tuition to the children of this house. Yes, for your kindness to us, we shall teach your children free of charge.

Act 2, Scene 1

(His friends look at him with discomfort at his unexpected promise.)

LAILA

Well, sirs, I'm not too sure we can help you since we don't even know the nature of your problem.

YABA

Besides, the only child in this house does not need a teacher. He is too ill at the moment to be taught anything.

AMY

Yes, my eight-year-old son is very ill and needs a doctor, not a teacher, to bring him back to good health. (She begins to sob.)

KENNY

But that is exactly our work! Don't cry, fine lady. We shall bring your sick son back to good health, for all three of us are doctors.
(DOLA and AYEH look at him with surprise as he silently appeals to them for their support.)

GIRLS

Doctors? But you just said you are teachers.

AYEH

So we said, but you see we used the word "teachers" metaphorically. We are actually doctors—all three of us.

DOLA
As doctors, we 'teach' the body to function correctly to the satisfaction and the general well-being of its owner.

KENNY *(happy it is going well)*
You see, a hospital is like a school and the doctor is like a teacher. The different parts of the body are the different pupils in a class and the drugs a doctor uses are like the teaching aids of a teacher.

GIRLS *(greatly impressed)*
Oh what a beautiful analogy!

LAILA
I'm surprised it never occurred to me to think of doctors as teachers.

YABA
Neither did I. Anyway, thank God you ended up in this house, for you are the very people we need here.

AMY
Welcome, sirs. Laila, please bring them water.

MEN *(disappointed, and to themselves)*
Water? *(to girls.)* Thank you for your kindness.

(Soft background music as LAILA serves them with water.)

KENNY
Thank you once again. By the way, what is wrong with the child?

AMY
Nyamekye, my eight year old child, became ill suddenly. I thought it was one of these short spells of fever we are all familiar with. But no, this one does not want to go. He has lost every appetite, has grown lean and his temperature is forever high.

DOLA
Has he seen any doctors?

AMY
Yes and he is on regular medication.

AYEH
Can we see his drugs, please?

AMY
Oh yes.
(Exit AMY to fetch the medications. She enters again quickly)

Here they are, sirs.

AYEH. *(inspects the drugs and passes them to his friends)*
Good, they are all very good, very useful drugs indeed.

KENNY *(returning the drugs to AMY)*
Anyway, we will not need them, for we have our own drugs,

(His colleagues are shocked at his claim.)

AYEH and DOLA *(forgetting themselves)*
We have? *(Then they hastily support KENNY's claim).* Oh, yes, we have some drugs with us.

KENNY
As doctors we never travel without our first aid box.

AYEH and DOLA
Our first aid box is our regular companion. You never know when it will come in handy.

AMY
This is what every conscientious doctor should do. Sirs, you are certainly dedicated doctors, and once again, you are most welcome.

LAILA.
Amy, I think you should let the good doctors know about your other children, too.

AYEH
Oh, you have other children apart from this sick one?

AMY
Yes, two of them, born after Nyamekye—but they are dead *(sobs)*.

MEN
Dead? We are very sorry. What happened?

AMY *(still crying)*
I don't know. They became ill and died. The boy after Nyamekye died when he was four and the girl when she was two.

KENNY *(moving to AMY)*
Don't cry, my pretty lady. Now that we are here, your problem is over. We shall do our best to save this one for you. So cheer up, all will be well.
(His two friends try hard to hide their discomfort, one coughing, the other wiping sweat off his face)

GIRLS
Thank you, O thank you, sirs. You have made us happy today.

KENNY
Can I go in and see the child?

DOLA and AYEH *(shocked at his request)*
What? You want to see the sick child?

AMY
Sure, sure, I'll take you in to see him right away.
(AMY and KENNY go in)

AYEH
Are the three of you sisters?

LAILA

No, we are friends, very good friends. Yaba and I came to assist Amy to look after Nyamekye, her sick child. In fact we come here almost every day to help Amy.

DOLA

And where is the child's father, if I may take a stranger's privilege to ask?

YABA

Oh sirs, you may not believe it, but he left them when the child fell ill.

MEN

Left when the child fell ill?

LAILA

Can you imagine that, sirs, a husband abandoning his wife and child when they needed him most?

AYEH

That is very wicked on his part.

YABA

It is such cruel behavior of some men that puts me off marriage. I pray that when I marry, my husband will not subject me to such callous treatment.

LAILA

So do I. I am not eager to enter into any marriage that will make me regret later. Amy married too quickly. She should have studied Teddy well before marrying him.

YABA

Don't blame Amy. Teddy wasn't bad at first. It is the pressure from various angles that has destroyed a good man.

AYEH and DOLA

Does that mean the two of you are not married?

LAILA and YABA

You heard us right, sirs. We are not married.

(Enter AMY and KENNY.)

LAILA

How did you find him, doctor?

KENNY

Well, the child is very ill; there is no doubt about that. But that is no problem to us. We have treated worse cases before.

AYEH and DOLA *(managing to control their surprise)*

We have? Oh, sure we have!

AMY

This is good news. I can't wait to see my dear child on his feet again. O good doctors, you have lifted up my drooping spirit and filled me with hope.

LAILA and YABA

Yes doctors, you are indeed God sent. We shall be very grateful to you if you help Nyamekye to enjoy normal life again.

MEN

Sure, we shall! Nyamekye will be well again in God's name.

GIRLS

Amen. Oh, thank you, good doctors. You have made us very happy today.

KENNY

Treating the boy is no problem. But before we do so we must eat, for we are very hungry. We've come a long way and we are starving.

DOLA and AYEH

Precisely. We need food, food, food!

GIRLS

Food?

MEN

Yes, for no man works on an empty stomach and right now, we are very hungry.

LAILA *(pulling the other GIRLS aside)*
Are you sure these are genuine doctors? Imagine doctors asking for food, like children, from people they hardly know. Besides, real doctors ask for fees before accepting any work, and not food!

YABA
You are right Laila, we shouldn't be in a hurry to trust them. There is something fishy about them. For all you know, they are fake doctors who are here to dupe us. I'm beginning to feel uncomfortable and suspicious. Men will never stop at taking advantage of unprotected, vulnerable girls.

AMY
I understand how you feel. Under normal circumstances we should not even entertain them. But I am desperate and I don't have a choice. I want my child to get better. Remember, a drowning man will cling to a straw. So please let's try them. There is no harm in trying.
(GIRLS continue to talk among themselves in low tones.)

DOLA *(pulling his friends aside, as the girls keep talking)*
Are you sure we are doing the right thing? Think about it. It may be dangerous and land us into trouble. Let's back out before it's too late.

KENNY
Don't be stupid, Dola.. Nothing ventured, nothing gained. How do we eat? How do we get help if we don't push ourselves? How long do you want us to remain in our misery?

DOLA
But not this particular push. This is too risky. Let's tell them the truth and see what happens.

KENNY
Don't take us back, Dola. We have already said that in our present predicament the truth will not help us. It will send us back to the street, the hot merciless street! Is that what we want?

DOLA
But we didn't know we would be involved with a sick child. Let's tell them the truth before it is too late. Remember, a life is at stake here, an innocent child's life.

AYEH
Shut up, Dola! What are you saying? To admit before these ladies that we are liars, fake, jobless? No! What sort of impression do you want them to form of us? No, Dola. I am not ready to bow down my head in shame before these pretty girls and walk away miserably from them. So long as we stay in this house we are learned doctors and I like that.

KENNY
Besides, we are not going to harm the poor boy. We are only here to get some food to eat. So what's your problem? Let us remain faithful to our chosen profession as doctors, get some food to eat, and go our way. Simple!

AMY

Err...kind doctors, we accept your proposition, but I have a small problem. You see, I don't have any food in the house at the moment.

MEN *(disappointed)*

What, no food in this house?

AMY

Neither do I have money on me to buy you food.

MEN

What, no money either?

AMY

But I'm expecting my mother home with some money any time from now.

MEN

And you want us to wait?

DOLA

This is too bad, it is a hopeless case. No food means no work. We are leaving.

GIRLS *(pleading)*

Oh please, don't go away.

KENNY

We can't work on empty stomachs. We are wasting time here. Brothers, let's leave.

GIRLS

Please sirs, don't go away. Stay and save the boy!

LAILA *(excitedly)*

But Amy, we can help you. We have food at home. After all, what are friends for?

YABA

Yes Amy, come with us. We have meat and fish and vegetables at home. We shall help you prepare a delicious meal for our special visitors right now.

LAILA

Kind sirs, we entreat you to stay and attend to Nyamekye. We shall be back soon with delicious food specially prepared for you.

MEN

No, we cannot work when we are hungry. We are leaving.

GIRLS *(pleading)*

Please don't go away, O good doctors.

MEN

We are going away, we cannot stay.

GIRLS
Do have mercy on us helpless women.

MEN
We are going away, we cannot work.

GIRLS
We shall do what you want, give us time, good sirs.
You have brought us some hope, don't leave now.

MEN
You better make it fast with the food, for we're starving.
Or we shall leave you and come back here no more.

GIRLS
Thank you sirs! We shall be back soon!

AMY
Wait a minute sirs, there is a basket of fruits a neighbour brought us this morning. You can have that for the time being. I'll get it for you.
(Exit AMY, returning with the basket of fruits.)

LAILA and YABA
Please do have some fruits while we rush home to prepare you something delicious.

MEN

Well, well, we shall have the fruits. But remember, we want proper food. Proper food will yield proper treatment. So hurry up and get us something good to eat.

GIRLS

Sure, sure we shall.

(Exit GIRLS, running.)

ACT II, SCENE 2

WITHERED HOPE

(The living room. The MEN are seated and sad.)

DOLA
That was a close shave! We nearly had it!

AYEH
I'm not sure we are off the hook yet.

KENNY
Oh cruel fate, what have you done to us, bringing us all the way here, to a home with no money, no food but only a sick child?

AYEH
As if our own misery is not enough. You bring us all the way to this house of pain to augment our over-brimmed sorrow. How on earth can we cure a sick child?

DOLA
Lord, we are in a very tight corner. Look at all the lies we have to concoct, all for a single, miserable banana. Kenny, is the child's condition as bad as you said?

KENNY
Do I even know? You go in and see for yourselves.
    (DOLA and AYEH go in. KENNY speaks to himself)

His lips are dry, eyes blank and cheeks hollow. The poor child may not survive. I'm not a doctor but when I see a hopeless case I know it.
    (Enter AYEH and DOLA.)

AYEH
Goodness gracious, what a mess we've put ourselves in! We can never treat this child, even if we were real doctors.

DOLA
Poor child! The girls must bring the food quickly for us to eat and leave this place fast.

AYEH
Meanwhile, what do we do?

KENNY
What do we do? We treat the boy!

DOLA

What? Treat the boy? How?

AYEH

You are not serious, Kenny. What treatment can we give?

KENNY

We shall treat the boy. Didn't we say we are doctors? Get me a glass of water; I'm going in to attend to him.

(KENNY goes in.)

DOLA

You can't be serious Kenny, since when did you become a medical officer?

(AYEH goes in with some water.)

And you too Ayeh, what are you going to do there? I won't go in again. I can't bear a second look at that pathetic figure on the bed. It is good I am not a doctor. Such sights make me feel uncomfortable and sad.

(Enter AYEH. He takes the fruit basket and exits.)

DOLA

Hey Ayeh, where are you going with the fruits? What are you two up to? You better make him well! Wait a minute. You are not eating the fruits in there without me!

(He charges for the door but stops.)

No, no, not even the fruits will make me enter that room a second time. Poor child, may the good Lord save him.
(Solemn music. DOLA is sitting alone sadly. After a while the OTHERS enter, wiping the sweat off their faces.)

DOLA *(anxiously)*
What is it? Is he alright? Will he be okay? Were you able to help him? Say something!

KENNY
Well, we've done what we could. We've forced some fluid down his system—water, and mixed fruit pulp. Though he ate it all, I wonder if it will do him any good. He opened his eyes as he ate and slept soon after that.

DOLA
That's good. At least you succeeded in feeding him.

AYEH
Yes, we did our best but he is too weak for my liking. One look at him and you know he doesn't stand a chance …
(A moan from within.)

AYEH and DOLA
What is that?

KENNY
I knew it. I knew it will come soon. It is the sound of the dying. They always do that when they are about to depart this world.

(KENNY goes in.)

AYEH

Oh my goodness, child, don't do this to us. Stay alive, for Christ's sake. You've no idea how much your existence means to us.

DOLA

Yes, hold on a little, dear child. We've waited so long for this moment to get something to eat. Your mother and her friends will be here soon with food for us. Please let us get our food and eat in peace.

(Enter KENNY.)

KENNY

It's no use. He is dying alright. Let's leave this place before the girls come back.

AYEH and DOLA

What? Leave this place on an empty stomach? No, Kenny, we are staying here for our food. We are too weak with hunger to walk away.

KENNY

The girls will not understand what you are saying when they find the boy dead. They will be sad, disappointed, angry and mad at us for giving them false hope. They will not give us food, don't you understand?

DOLA

Why won't they give us food when they have promised to do so? That will be a breach of promise.

KENNY

It will be a breach of nothing. Didn't we also promise to cure the boy, and have we done that? Besides, you cannot argue with a woman in grief, a woman who has lost a child. Let us leave this place quickly before the girls come and have us arrested and thrown in jail.

DOLA

No! I am not leaving. I won't move an inch from this place. Remember it was hunger that brought us here and until I eat I won't leave this place.

(He sits down.)

KENNY

For goodness' sake, Dola, forget about food and use your head for once!

AYEH

No, Kenny, the case is not as simple as you make it sound. You see, if it were just a case of food we could forget, but it is a matter of the heart as well. I am in love. I am hooked and I'm not leaving this place.

(He sits down.)

KENNY

Are you crazy? How can you sit there and talk of love when you stand in danger of losing your life?

(He pulls him up.)

DOLA

Don't waste your time, Kenny. You cannot argue with a man in love.

AYEH

Oh, I am smitten by a woman's beauty!
I am in love with a charming lady!
My life's river has found its source.
My happiness resides in this house.
And so here I stay for the rest of my days,
No matter what the whole world says.

(He sits down.)

KENNY

No, we can't stay here, not for love or for food they've promised us. What's wrong with the two of you? Can't you see that if the girls come and find that the child is dead there will be trouble for us? Not food, not love but trouble, big, big trouble will be our lot!

AYEH

But the child is not dead, so why must we run away? And even if he dies we cannot be held responsible for that. The boy was dying long before we came in and they all know that.

KENNY

Tell them that when they come! Listen, Ayeh, much as we all want to stay here and enjoy the food and the company of these pretty ladies, common sense tells us that we cannot. They will not look kindly on us when they discover that the child is dead.

DOLA and AYEH

But the child is not dead!

KENNY

But he is dying. How many times should I repeat that? He may die any moment from now. Can't you see? Let's leave now.

DOLA

And you want us to go back into the street and say goodbye to the food they've gone to prepare for us, the comfort and happiness that are about to come our way?

KENNY

Unfortunately so.

AYEH

Oh what an irony of life! What twisted fate! Now that food is almost within our reach, food specially prepared for us, we have to run away from it. Must we turn our back on the very things we desire most in life? For how long are we going to succumb to misery and frustration, Lord, for how long?
Why do you do this to us, Lord?

You raise our hopes one minute and crush our dreams the next. Why, Lord, why?

KENNY

I can't answer that but what I can tell you is that we've got to pack ourselves out of this house right now before it is too late.

(A moan from within)

Ah . . . the sound of the dying again. The child is well on his way out. Let's be quick and quit this place before the girls come. I'll get our tools.

(Exit KENNY.)

DOLA *(reluctantly getting up)*

Goodbye comfort, goodbye happiness, goodbye food. It hurts to leave without filling our stomachs. It hurts very much to walk away on an empty stomach into the hot, unfriendly street again.

AYEH *(reluctantly getting up)*

Goodbye, sweet ladies, goodbye, love. You will never know how much we have wanted to stay here and comfort you, share your grief and be part of your life. Oh, this life is hard, this life is harsh.

(Enter KENNY with their tools.)

KENNY *(solemnly)*

It is not our wish to leave you, dear child, but we have no choice but to leave. But before we go, my brothers, let's pray.

(They hold hands.)

Dear Father in heaven, we leave everything in your merciful hands. Great physician, mighty healer, it is not too late for you to save Nyamekye from the clutches of death and make him strong again. We believe and trust that you can save Nyamekye.. Save him, Lord, save this dear child from death. Thank you, Lord, for hearing our prayer. Amen.

AYEH

Dear God, give Amy and her friends strength to take care of Nyamekye.. Take away their pain, fears, suffering and worries and fill this house with peace and happiness once more.

DOLA

Divine Pilot, as we step out of this house, let us step not into any trouble. But steer us safely to your realm of light and love, peace and prosperity where we will work hard and serve you with all our strength and with all our hearts. Amen

ALL

Amen!
Goodbye dear child, goodbye sweet girls,
Back to the sad street we must go.
Goodbye shelter, food and comfort.
Back to the sad street we must go.
Welcome misery, welcome harsh life.
Welcome sorrow, pain and struggle.
Back to the sad street we must go.

(Exit all. Solemn music. Enter NYAMEKYE.)

NYAMEKYE
Where is everybody? Father, Mother, Grandmother, where are you? See, I am well; I am well!

(Exit NYAMEKYE, calling "Mother, mother! Father!")

ACT III, SCENE 1

CHEERING RAY

(Same setting. Enter AMY, LAILA and YABA, briskly with baskets of food and drinks, very happy thinking the doctors are busy inside working on the sick child. They set the food and drinks on the dining table.)

GIRLS

Sirs, your food is ready. We have brought you delicious food.
We have come to serve you,
O doctors great, divinely sent.
Gifts of food we offer
Since you're from far away.
Soups and stews so tasty,
With well- spiced meat and fish,
Fries and fruits of all kinds,
We serve you with all our hearts.

AMY

Good sirs, your meal is ready.

LAILA

Please good doctors, give yourselves a break and have a bite, for meals are best enjoyed when they are warm.

YABA

Besides, you need energy to tackle the work at hand, for man must not work on an empty stomach, as you rightly said.

GIRLS

What, no response? This is strange.

YABA

Let's go in and see.

LAILA

No, no, let them work. Let them cure Nyamekye, please.

AMY

But…but…Are these not the doctors who were threatening to leave because of hunger?

YABA

And would not work in spite of our pleadings?

LAILA

Yes, the very ones. But they are enjoying their work so much that not even our food, deliciously prepared, will pull them away from what they are doing inside. Their great love for their work has subdued their hunger. Good job, doctors, good job.

Act 3, Scene 1

Carry on!

(They wait a little while.)

ALL *(sing)*
Soups and stews so tasty
With well-spiced meat and fish
Fries and fruits of all kinds
We serve you with all our hearts.

AMY
Are you sure they are in? I can't hear any sound. Wait, I'll go in and find out.

(LAILA stops her.)

LAILA
No Amy, don't go there. Do you want Nyamekye to get better? Then for the child's sake, don't disturb them. Let them work in peace.

AMY
But I'm not at peace. My heart is troubled. Something tells me that I must go and see what is happening inside. I guess it's a mother's instinct. Yes, I'll go in and tell them politely that their food is ready.

(AMY goes in. She is heard screaming and re-enters.)

Oh no, they are not in. They are gone, gone! And Nyamekye too. They've kidnapped my son! My son is also gone! *(She weeps.)*

YABA and LAILA
What! Gone? Where did they go? Nyamekye too gone?

YABA
Oh God, what is the meaning of this? Why would anybody kidnap a sick child?

LAILA
Ask that again! We shouldn't have left them alone with Nyamekye in the first place. Three total strangers! We should have known better.

YABA
But in our peculiar situation what could we have done, but to trust them. We were desperate and too eager to get them to treat Nyamekye.

AMY *(still sobbing)*
Oh my son, my son, what have they done to you? Where have they taken you, my son?
(She walks towards the entrance.)

Where are you, Nyamekye?

OTHERS
How can we find you, Nyamekye? Where do we go? Shall we go this way or shall we move that way?

ALL *(sing solemnly)*
How can we find you, oh dear child,
When tears have blinded our eyesight?
We need a hand to show us the way
That will lead us to where you are.

NYAMEKYE *(sings briskly offstage)*
Mother, mother wipe your tears now.
See, your child is fit and strong and well again.
Mother, mother wipe your tears now.
For your child is fit and strong.
Sing and shout for joy, oh mother!
For your son is fit and strong again,
He's fit and strong again!

AMY
Listen! Isn't that Nyamekye's voice?

OTHERS
No, It can't be. Nyamekye is too weak to be out there singing.

AMY
But the voice, it sounds very much like Nyamekye's voice. Let's move in the direction of the voice and see what happens.
(They sing "How can we find you ... " and Nyamekye sings back "Mother wipe your tears" and enters.)

GIRLS *(excited)*
It's him, it's Nyamekye! He is strong. O Nyamekye! Thank God!

(NYAMEKYE moves into the warm embrace of his mother and her friends.)

AMY

Is that really you, my son? What happened to you? Tell me, tell me everything. How do you feel? Are you alright?

NYAMEKYE

Yes, mother I am well. It was all like a dream. It was as if I was on a long journey; all was dark and silent. Then suddenly I saw some strange men, two or three of them, hovering over me. I could not see them well because of the darkness. But they spoke kindly to me, prayed for me and gave me to eat and drink. Then I fell into a deep sleep. When I finally woke up the darkness had gone and there was light. The men too had gone. You and Father were not in, neither was grandmother. I got out of bed, walked around a little and went out to look for you. I did not find you so I decided to come back home and wait for you. So here I am, mother. See, I am strong again.

(NYAMEKYE sings and dances, joined by AMY and her friends.)

NYAMEKYE

I can move my arms about,
And I can move my legs too.
I can sway from left to right,
And turn myself around too.
I can flip and flit and hop.
I can twist my body.
So I sing and dance with joy,
To tell the world I'm healthy.

GIRLS

So we sing and dance with joy
To thank the Lord for His Mercy.

NYAMEKYE

I can see the bright blue sky
And I can smell the flowers.
I can hear the birds sing sweetly
And fill the world with gladness.
I can feel the fresh breeze blow
On every part of my being.
So I sing and dance with joy
To tell the world I'm happy.

GIRLS

So we sing and dance with joy
To thank the Lord for His Mercy.

AMY

I thank you, God for Nyamekye's recovery. Oh, I'm very happy, Nyamekye, for your recovery has made me strong again. You've made me a woman again and restored my confidence. I can once more hold my head up among my fellow women.

NYAMEKYE

Where is Father, mother? I want him to see that I am well.

AMY

In due course, my son, you shall see him. By the way, Nyamekye, where are the doctors who were here with you?

NYAMEKYE
Doctors? There was nobody with me when I woke up. I was alone in the room and in the house.

AMY
Alone in the house? But we left you in the care of three doctors, three great doctors. Where are they? We thought they left with you.

NYAMEKYE
No, nobody was with me, nobody went out with me. I was all alone.

YABA
Perhaps they've gone to look for food. Didn't they say they were very hungry? We must have delayed in bringing them food and they couldn't control their hunger any more.

LAILA
So they've probably gone in search of food. Oh no! We must stop them. We have better food here for them, food prepared with true hearts and loyal hands, food that will be served with warmth, affection and respect.

YABA
Oh such learned men, talented scholars, yet so unassuming and so ordinary. The very epitome of humility! We must find them and hail them the heroes of the day.

NYAMEKYE
Who are these doctors and where do they come from, mother?

AMY
Nyamekye, my son, we don't know where these doctors came from. We don't even know their names. But it was as if they were specially sent from Heaven to come and save you. I don't know what would have happened to you if these doctors had not appeared on the scene at the time they did.

NYAMEKYE.
So I owe my life to them? Great doctors, oh how I wish I could see you and thank you for saving my life.

AMY
So you shall, my son. We shall certainly search everywhere till we find these good doctors and thank them for saving your life.

YABA
They deserve to be rewarded. Conquerors of a disease that has defied all treatment. Masters of medicine, come and get your praise.

LAILA
Mighty healers, great doctors we shall surely search for you, find you and thank you, honour you and…love you?

AMY and YABA
What did you say, Laila, love them?

LAILA

Yes, love them! What is wrong with that? Are they not the type of men we've been waiting for? Are they not our dream partners? Men of action, not words, steeped in simplicity and humility who scorn flamboyance and ostentation. Are these not men of our hearts?

YABA

You are right, Laila, you are right. They are the type of men we admire. For the first time the love strings of my heart have been set vibrating. Great doctors, who will not boast of their high social standing, learned men who are so meek and plain like the lowly placed common man, come and get your praise. Oh, you are indeed men of our hearts.

AMY

They are full of love and compassion. They treated my boy without charging any fee while those doctors who collected huge fees failed to cure him. Oh, these are truly men of our hearts.

LAILA

It is amazing! All that they asked for was food, food, the basic need of all humanity. But we shall give them more than food. We shall give them our hearts, our love and our lives.

YABA

Quick, let's pack the food and go and search for them.

(They pack the food.)

GIRLS *(sing)*
We are ready to hail you,
O doctors great divinely sent.
Sweetest love we offer
Since you're so kind and true.
Doctors great and humble,
We give our hearts to you.
We'll spread the joyful tidings.
We'll spread them far away.

AMY

The whole town must hear of this. Come, let's go after them. We must not let them slip away.

YABA

No, they must not slip away. That will be most unfortunate. Let's hurry up and find them fast. Let's go!

NYAMEKYE

Am I coming along too?

AMY

Of course you are coming along with us, my child. We won't let you out of our sight for anything.

GIRLS

Come, Nyamekye, let's go and search for the doctors and spread the news of your recovery.

(Sing)

We are ready to hail you,
O doctors great divinely sent.
Sweetest love we offer,
Since you're so kind and true.
Doctors great and humble,
We give our hearts to you.
We'll spread the joyful tidings.
We'll spread them far away.

(Exit all, singing and dancing.)

ACT III, SCENE 2

SWEET SOUNDS

───────────────

(Living room of MAA BEA.. Enter MAA BEA., tired but happy. Goes to pour herself water, sits down, talking, thinking AMY is inside with NYAMEKYE.)

───────────────

MAA BEA *(excitedly)*

Amy, I'm back. I told you God will provide. I was able to sell everything. Come and see, my purse is full again. God has a way of taking care of the widow and the fatherless. I told you when He closes one door He opens another. Now I have enough money to take care of all our needs. We don't have to worry anymore. At least not now. Amy, Amy. Oh, so I've been speaking to myself. She must be tired and sleeping. Poor girl, I don't blame her. She is going through a very tough moment.

(MAA BEA goes in. She re-enters, agitated.)

Oh my goodness, they are not in. Where are they? No, no, it can't be. I shouldn't have left them alone. Please God, let no

harm come to them. Oh Nyamekye, after all our efforts to save you? Oh, no, no. *(She breaks down crying.)*
(Enter AWO and AYA beautifully dressed, talking about a meeting they attended.)

AWO

Hello Maa Bea! The meeting was great, Maa Bea. It was a pity you couldn't make it.

AYA

I was impressed by today's attendance. Almost everybody was there. Look Awo, Maa Bea is crying. I'm sure she is still upset by Teddy's cruelty to Amy.

AWO

Stop crying, Maa Bea. Don't let Teddy's cruelty eat your heart. It's not good for your health.

AYA

You must stay strong for Amy. You know you are her pillar and her rock here. So be strong for her. Don't cry.

MAA BEA

I'm not crying because of Teddy. *(She cries harder.)*

OTHERS

It's not Teddy? What is it then? What makes you cry so much? Is it Nyamekye?

MAA BEA

Yes!

AWO and AYA

Oh God! What happened? What's wrong with Nyamekye? Don't tell us he is…

MAA BEA

No, I can't tell you that because I don't know.

AYA

So why are you crying, Maa Bea? We don't understand. Tell us what happened.

MAA BEA

You see, I left Amy here to look after the child while I took a short trip next town to look for money to run the house.

AYA

Just look at that! Teddy, the father of Nyamekye, has all the money one can imagine and yet he will not provide money for the recovery of his own sick child.

AWO

Oh my sister you speak as if you don't know what men do when they become rich. They don't think of sick children, they think of taking on new wives. Tell us your story, Maa Bea. What happened?

MAA BEA

I got home not long ago to find the house empty. The children are not in. Oh Bea, this is my misfortune. To think it happened in my absence. To think I was not around when they needed me most. I'm sure they are at the hospital now. Please, take me to the hospital.

AYA *(wiping a tear)*

Stop crying, Maa Bea. Have faith. You have been a tower of strength to Amy, all this time. Keep it up, for she needs you now more than ever. You don't have to meet the poor girl with tears. You'll make it hard for her, so wipe away your tears.

AWO

Oh God, please don't let Amy lose this child too, for that will be a heavy cross indeed for her to bear.

AYA

Maa Bea, leave all to God. The Lord we do serve is merciful and will take full control of every situation.

MAA BEA

Thank you, my friends. You do fill me with courage. Let's go to the hospital now. I'm sure I'll find Amy there with your daughters.

AWO

Our daughters? You mean Laila and Yaba? Were they here with Amy?

MAA BEA
Yes, they were with Amy when she brought me my purse at the station and they promised to come home with her and help her look after Nyamekye...

AYA *(excitedly)*
That's it! I can guess where they are. Cheer up, Maa Bea. Amy and the child are with her friends at either my place or at Awo's place. Our daughters must have coaxed Amy into coming along with them and taking the sick child as well, when they saw you were away.

MAA BEA
But how did they manage that? Nyamekye is very weak.

AYA
Trust Yaba and Laila. They are two of a kind. Very strong-willed and determined girls. They know exactly how to get what they want. They must have convinced Amy that a change of environment will do them good.

MAA BEA *(brightening up)*
That is very possible. Why didn't I think about this? O, this is very comforting. I feel better already. Thank you very much. You are such wonderful friends, supporting me in my most trying moments.

AYA
That is what friendship is all about—to help one another in times of difficulty.

MAA BEA

Come, let's go and look for the children at your place.

AWO

No, Maa Bea. You stay here and rest. Aya will keep you company. I'll go alone and check on the children. I'll be back soon with them. I'm sure I will. Just relax and wait for me.

MAA BEA

It will not be easy for me to sit here and wait. Let me go with you, please. *(She gets up.)*

AYA

No Maa Bea. You are staying here with me.
(AYA holds MAA BEA to her chair while AWO walks to the door.)

AWO

I can see a man coming from the distance towards this house.

MAA BEA

Is he somebody we know?
(She attempts to get up but AYA pulls her down gently.)

AWO

I'm not sure, but from the way he is walking and the look in his eyes he seems to have some urgent message for us. I'll wait to hear his news before I go.

AYA

What news is he bringing? What could be the matter?

MAA BEA

It's obvious, isn't it? What urgent news can it be? The child is gone, gone, gone!
(A funeral dirge on flute is heard offstage. All three women break down in tears as they speak.)

MAA BEA

O, Nyamekye, you have dealt us a terrible blow and plunged us in deep sorrow. The only egg in the nest is also broken? Our young master, our budding scholar, our gentleman, our one and only, you have also fallen asleep when night is far away. You have fallen asleep to wake no more. Why, oh why must this happen to us?

AYA

Nyamekye, you are free from pain and suffering. You are no more part of our struggling world. Nothing can harm you again. Earthly fathers can do their worst but your heavenly Father will never forsake you! Rest peacefully in His bosom, my child, sleep well.

AWO

Farewell Nyamekye, take our condolence. You have finished the race at the beginning, condolence. Your sun has set at noon, Nyamekye, leaving us to grope in the darkness of the day. Oh when shall we have another like you to cheer us up?

AYA

Sisters, I can hear his footsteps. The man is almost here. Let's wipe our tears quickly and hear what news he has for us.
(They wipe their tears, and sit ready for the visitor.)
(Enter a MAN.)

MAN

Good day, my mothers. I am only a messenger, sent to see if the good woman of this house, Maa Bea, is back from her journey, and to give her the news.

MAA BEA

I am home, my son. So it is true. It is true about Nyamekye?

MAN

Sure it is. Every word of it is true.

MAA BEA

Oh my God, why? Why should this happen to us?
(The women wail. MAA BEA falls on her two friends who, crying, help her to sit up.)

MAN *(shocked)*

What a strange way of expressing joy!

AWO

I beg your pardon?

MAN

I said you people amaze me with your strange way of expressing happiness. Tears of joy I know of, but serious wailing and grieving in the name of joy, I'm yet to come across.

AYA

How can you talk of joy in the midst of death? Don't you have any respect for the dead?

AWO

What do you expect us to do? Why should we rejoice when our source of joy is dead? How can we be happy? Perhaps you can teach us how to do that.

MAN

Dead? Who is dead? I don't know of any death.

MAA BEA

Is Nyamekye, my grandson, not dead?

MAN

God forbid! No! Who said Nyamekye is dead? Nyamekye is very much alive and feeling fine. In fact, that's why I was sent here to prepare you for the happy news.

WOMEN

Nyamekye, alive and well?

MAA BEA

Oh my poor heart, swinging from one extreme state of emotion to another.

(To MAN) Good sir, did you say Nyamekye, my grandson, is alive and well?

MAN

Yes, he is. Nyamekye your grandson is alive and very well.

MAA BEA

And did you see him walking on his own two feet?

MAN

Not only was he walking on his two feet, he was actually dancing!

WOMEN

What? Nyamekye dancing? Then today will be our dancing day too.

(They begin to sing and dance.)

Today shall be our dancing day,
When we shall dance from street to street,
To tell the world what God has done,
For God has wiped away our tears!

WOMEN

And now tell us, how did Nyamekye regain his health, and where is he and his mother?

AYA and AWO
And our daughters Yaba and Laila, where are they?

MAN
It is a long story but you shall hear it all. You will soon know all that happened. Right now the whole town is rejoicing at Nyamekye's sudden recovery. Women spread their best cloths before him and the great doctors who saved his life, while others shower gifts of all kinds on them.

MAA BEA
Great doctors? Which great doctors are you talking about? I must say a lot has indeed happened in my short absence. Tell us more, young man, for you bring sweet news indeed.

AYA
Yes, these doctors who treated Nyamekye, who are they and where did they come from?

MAN
They are three talented doctors who came from afar and who in all humility have refused to be addressed as doctors…

WOMEN
Have refused to be called doctors?

MAN
Yes, but I am happy to announce that these great doctors who have refused to be addressed as doctors are now your sons.

WOMEN

Our sons, what do you mean?

MAN

Nature took its course. For no sooner had the two parties met than love so strong and pure joined the hearts and hands of your three daughters and those of the three doctors in a knot so firmly tied that nothing can untie it. In short, your daughters and the doctors are ready to be joined in holy matrimony any moment from now.

WOMEN

Our daughters getting married? That fast? Children of today can be fast on such matters.

MAN

But very understanding in this particular case. You would have done the same if you were in their shoes.

AYA

Bet we would! Only God knows the number of times we've been on our knees, praying for this day to come.

AWO

And today is the day the Lord has appointed for our girls to be married. Can you believe that? Oh God, you are so good, so wonderful and we give you all glory and praise.

MAA BEA

Yes my sisters, God's time, they say, is the best. And this is the day the Lord has made. So what are we standing here for? Let us rejoice and be glad in it. Oh yes, let's dance for joy as we thank God for what He has done for us.

ALL

Today shall be our dancing day,
When we shall dance from street to street,
To tell the world what God has done
For God has wiped away our tears.

WOMEN

Please, sir, go on with your sweet story. We can't wait to hear it all and sip the sweetness from it.

MAN

And as a sign of his deep appreciation for what the doctors had done, our great ruler himself, in addition to the many gifts and blessings already bestowed on them, released a sizeable portion of his land to the doctors saying, "Stay and be part of us. You will not only marry these, our three daughters, but we will also build a clinic here for you so that you can treat the sick in this town."

WOMEN

O gracious father of the nation, benevolent one, great provider, and supporter of the needy how can we fully thank you?

MAA BEA
We shall help build the clinic in every possible way we can.

MAN
But that will never be. For our august visitors, now your sons, seem to have had their fill of medicine, and will never go to it again. Instead they've decided to go into farming! Well, who knows what they may become next when they finish with farming.

WOMEN
This is very interesting. Doctors turned farmers?

AWO
Isn't that what we want? Gifted and versatile young men who can easily swing from one profession to another. Our daughters could not have made a better choice.

AYA
And what do our girls themselves say about their doctors becoming farmers? Are they happy with this sudden change of profession?

MAN
As happy as queens, I must say. You should see them beside their husbands, beaming with smiles that speak of total contentment. For according to your daughters they are marrying their husbands for who they are and not what they are. They will love

them no matter what work they do, provided it's decent and honest.

MAA BEA
O God, your ways are wonderful. Nyamekye, who a short while ago was at the point of death, is now fit and strong, and Amy, whose husband painfully abandoned her, is once again a happy wife. Let me go and get ready for this happy occasion.

(MAA BEA goes in)

AYA
And at last, my Laila has got a man of her heart. I know my daughter; her head is firmly fixed on her neck. She will not rush into any union that will bring regret later.

AWO
And my Yaba too, ever so sensible and cautious, has at last found her soul mate. Oh, I am so happy for them, our girls, our sons-in-law. Where are they now? I can't wait to see them.

MAN
After feasting at the royal palace with our great ruler himself, they are on their way here to receive your blessing before the final one in the church.

WOMEN
Thank you very much, sir, for bringing us the sweetest news our ears have received in recent times.

(Enter MAA BEA, beautifully dressed, holding extra shawls for her friends.)

MAA BEA

Here, get these, my sisters, and let us be ready to receive them and be part of this special moment. Our weeping is over, our fears have vanished and our joy knows no end.

ACT III, SCENE 3

BRIGHTEST AND BEST

(Background music "Here Comes the Bride.". The couples, beautifully dressed, led by NYAMEKYE as page boy, slowly enter in pairs: AMY and KENNY, AYEH and YABA and DOLA and LAILA. They embrace the three mothers as they get to them in turns.)

NYAMEKYE
Where is my father? I can't see him here. Will someone please tell me where my father is?

AMY
In due course, my son, you shall be told.

MAA BEA
My sons, news of your greatness has long reached us and we know why you are here with our daughters. Words are too feeble to express our great delight and the depth of our gratitude

to you. We gladly offer our daughters' hands to you. We ask God's blessings upon your marriages. May you remain faithful through all the changing scenes of life, for a true husband is one who sticks to his wife and children all the time, in sickness and in health. He doesn't run away in the face of crisis. For crisis is a learning period, a test time. How you handle it will bring either the best out of you or the worst.

AYA

And you my daughters, marriage is not just the beautiful dress you wear. It is more serious, deep and sacred. You don't enter it anyhow and leave. Marriage is for keeps. Hold fast to your husbands, respect and honour them. Share your joys and sorrows, trust each other completely and keep no secrets between you. Besides, take time off your busy schedules and spend quality time together. Never be slaves to stress and fatigue. Enjoy your marriage.

AWO

But above all, my children, remember to place God at the centre of your marriage. Call upon Him always to direct all your ways. Pray to Him for strength and wisdom to enable you serve Him well, for with God all things are possible. You can face your fears and overcome your storms.

KENNY

Thank you very much, dear mothers, for your sound advice, kind words and wonderful reception. It seems as if we have known your daughters all our lives. In this short space of time, we have learnt a lot about them. They are really beautiful in every sense of the word, and we love them dearly. In fact, they mean a whole world to us.

AYEH

Yes, your daughters are the embodiment of beauty in its totality and they won our respect and love the moment we got to know them. In fact, our love is mutual and reciprocal.

DOLA

Oh yes, our coming together was so magical and so divine. It was obvious God himself directed us straight to our wives. And I want to assure you that we are going to nurture and cherish this love planted in us by the Almighty God Himself for the rest of our lives.

MAA BEA

You are right, my sons. Your coming into the lives of our daughters was indeed a divine intervention that brought an end to all our pains and sufferings. It was like a breath of fresh air that we truly needed here.

KENNY

It may interest you all to know that not long ago we were in the same sad boat as you. We too have had our fair share of a very difficult moment. We were physically, psychologically and emotionally unwell...

GIRLS

You were unwell? All three of you?

KENNY

Yes, all three of us. We were totally down and devastated. Our spirits were so low that we thought we had reached our end.

GIRLS

What happened? Tell us, please.

AYEH

Sure, you will hear every detail of our story, since you are now part of us. We will tell you everything. There will never be any secrets between us.

DOLA

But for the time being, let's just say that God in his miraculous and mysterious way which man can never understand, has healed us and lifted us up.

AYEH

And now look at us, swimming in happiness. We now have plots of land at our disposal to work on. We have our lovely wives and our precious son Nyamekye who will always occupy a special place in our hearts.

KENNY and DOLA

Yes, Nyamekye shall forever be our very special child in sickness or in health.

NYAMEKYE

Thank you very much. But I want to know where my father is.

I want to see him.

MAA BEA

You will know where your father is as your mother promised you, and you will see him. But for the time being let's be grateful to God for what He has done for us.

(Solemn background music. Enter TEDDY.)

NYAMEKYE.

Father, oh Father, where have you been all this time? Why have you not been here with us?

(He moves towards TEDDY but is held back by AMY.)

TEDDY *(sings solemnly and tearfully)*

"With broken heart and contrite heart,
A trembling sinner, Lord I cry.
Thy pardoning grace is rich and free;
O God, be merciful to me."

NYAMEKYE

Where were you, Father? Where did you go? I've been waiting all this time to see you, but Father you were nowhere to be seen.

TEDDY *(sings)*

"I smite upon my troubled heart
With deep and conscious guilt oppressed.
Christ and his cross my only plea.
O God, be merciful to me."

NYAMEKYE

Don't you love us and care for us anymore, Father? Don't you want to be with me and Mother anymore? Don't you want us to be happy as we used to be?

TEDDY *(sings)*

"Far off I stand with tearful eyes.
Nor dare uplift them to the Lord.
But thou dost all my anguish see.
O God, be merciful to me."

NYAMEKYE

Why are you crying, Father? Look, Father I'm well again and everybody is happy for me. Why are you not happy like everyone else? Why are you so sad? Why do you make me feel sad, Father?

TEDDY

One never appreciates or values what he has until he loses it. I bow my head in shame. The weight of my sin is heavy on me, my son. I cannot sleep at night; neither can I eat at day. I have wronged you, Nyamekye. I have wronged you, Amy. I miss your thoughtfulness, your devotion and your generosity.

(He kneels before AMY and NYAMEKYE.)

Please forgive me and come back to me. "Thy pardoning Grace is my only plea, Oh God be merciful to me."

AMY *(helps him up)*
Get up, Teddy! What are you doing here? What do you want from me and my son, Teddy?

NYAMEKYE
Don't say that, Mother. Why are you speaking like that to my father?

TEDDY
Your mother is right, son; I don't deserve to be here, my son. I left your mother for another woman. But she too has left me. Please come back to me, Amy.

NYAMEKYE
Why Father, why did you do that? *(He begins to cry.)*

AMY
Don't cry, Nyamekye my son, don't cry. This man here does not deserve your tears.

AYA
And why did the woman you married leave you, if I may ask?

TEDDY
She left me the moment she discovered the two of us belonged to the same blood group–A.S.

MAA BEA

And what is wrong with the two of you being A.S.? Why should that make her leave you?

TEDDY

That's why I feel so guilty and ashamed. If I had done this long ago I would have saved us this unpleasant situation. You see Amy and I are both A.S. This means the possibility of some of our children being S.S. is very high.

AWO

S.S.? What is S.S?

TEDDY

How do I explain it? Let me just say they are sickle cells, a type of blood cell, and people with S.S. have inherited blood disorder. They are often anaemic, jaundiced, tired, weak and have joint pains. They are delicate and need special care. They cannot stand a lot of things. Our two children died because they were both sicklers and could not survive the crisis they had.

NYAMEKYE

Am I also S.S.?

TEDDY

No, my son, you are A.S. like your mother and me.

KENNY

And I am A.A., Amy.

AMY

Thank God.

(AMY hugs KENNY, thanking God.)

MAA BEA

Thank you God, thank you for the blessings you have bestowed on us. Teddy, why are you now telling us all this? Where were you when your people were accusing Amy of being abnormal, unusual and a witch of a wife who kills her own children? Where were you?

AWO

Yes, Teddy, if you know all this about SSS and JSS why didn't you tell your people, especially your mother Afi, that it was SSS that killed your children and not Amy? Why didn't you defend Amy?

AYA

Rather, you stood there enjoying the scene, enjoying the humiliation and pain Amy was going through.

AMY

And when you finally spoke, all you could say was, you agreed totally with your people. I still remember vividly all that you said. Your words were like a dagger cutting me into pieces. I could not believe my ears. Yet there you stood in flesh and blood, uttering those cruel words. I cried to you to take me back, but you did not hear me. I offered you my love, but you rejected it and scorned me. I entreated you to stay with your sick child, but you turned your back on him too. What do you want from us now, Teddy? What do you want?

NYAMEKYE

Is that true, Father? Did you abandon us? Did you turn your back on us?

LAILA

Yes, it is true, Nyamekye, as true as the air we breathe. Your father left you and your mother when you became seriously ill and needed him most.

NYAMEKYE

Why, Father? Why did you do that?

YABA

Nyamekye, this is the bitter and painful truth we could not tell you. How could we tell you that your own father didn't want you and your mother in his life again when you fell ill? But now, you know it all.

TEDDY

I know what I did was wrong, and I'm very sorry but please hear me out. I have not finished yet.

YABA

What more do you have to say that will change the situation?

Don't bother, Teddy, we are not interested. When the storm was fierce and strong, you stayed away. Now that it is all over, and there is peace and call all around, you have suddenly appeared here. What for? We don't need you. Please leave us alone. Your tears and apology have come too late.

MAA BEA

I know how you all feel, but let's listen to him.

LAILA

But Maa Bea, is that necessary at all?

MAA BEA

Yes it is. We have a lot to learn from such mistakes and experiences as we travel along life. You have just begun a new journey, and you need such lessons to guide and guard you along.

MAN

Maa Bea says we must hear him so we shall. Speak, Teddy. We are listening.

TEDDY

Thank you, good people. You see, when our two children died, I did not bother to read the post-mortem report, for according to my mother it would not bring the dead back to life, but would only worsen my grief. It was only when Amy and I separated that I read the report and discovered for the first time what actually killed the children. And when my new wife, who is also A.S. saw that, she left me.

YABA

Of course. What do you expect? Knowing what you did to Amy, why should she stay to suffer the same fate?

MAA BEA

Teddy, you remember I advised you to reconsider your decision, for hasty actions often lead to later regret?

TEDDY

You did, Maa Bea, you did.

MAA BEA

Anyway, I'm glad you have realised your own mistake and have come to apologise. There is comfort in that. By the way, are your people aware of where you are now and what you are doing?

TEDDY

Yes. In fact, they will join me here any moment to ask for pardon. Ah, they are already here.
(Enter AFI leading her team in, singing solemnly.)

AFI and OTHERS

We have come to take you home, O woman true and kind.
We have done you grievous wrong O woman true and kind.
Wipe your tears, precious one.
Take your things and come with us.
We should never have sent you away.
We shall never, never let you out of our sight again.

MAA BEA
What brings you here, good people?

1ST ELDER
Our mission here today is one of peace and reconciliation.

2ND ELDER
I'm sure you remember that not too long ago we came here to …

AFI
Who cares for the past? We are not here to dig up the past and spread unwanted debris around. Don't beat about the bush as you always do. Just go straight to the point and tell them why we are here.

ELDERS
Afi! Afi!

1ST ELDER
What is wrong with you, Afi? Why can't you exercise a little patience? You are always rushing, and in your rush you destroy a lot of things.

2ND ELDER
Afi, if you had exercised a little patience and advised your son against his hasty decision, we wouldn't be here on this shameful mission!

AFI

Shameful? What is shameful about coming to take home our own wife? Have you forgotten how she wept bitterly when we asked her to stay away from Teddy? Do you call that happiness? So if we are here to take her back to where her happiness lies, what is shameful about that? Tell me.

2ND ELDER

Everything, everything. That is not how to handle such a delicate case. If I had known this is how you were going to behave, I wouldn't have followed you.

AFI

Never mind. I can handle it myself. Maa Bea, we are here to take Amy home. Teddy her husband needs her home. So Amy, my daughter, go pack your things and let's go home.

LAILA and YABA

Go home? Which home? You are not serious, Maa Afi.

MAA BEA

Afi, you have always been a smart woman …

AFI *(pleased)*

Yes, there is no doubt about that. Everybody says I am very smart.

MAA BEA

But not this time. You are too late Afi, for Amy my daughter now belongs to someone else, a man who knows her worth and appreciates her a lot.

AFI

Impossible! That can't be. Amy was… er … is Teddy's wife. She can't belong to another man just like that.

TEDDY

Mother, please stay out of this.

AFI

How can I, Teddy my son, how can I stay out? See how you are begging and pleading, and no one seems to care? They all know that it is not easy for a man to kneel before a woman to beg for forgiveness, yet you bravely do that and nobody is moved, not even Amy who claims to love you.

TEDDY

Mother, what are you saying? Were you not the one who forced me to leave Amy because you claimed she was not suitable for me? Have you forgotten the number of times you came to me day and night, insisting that my marriage to Amy was all a mistake, and that you would look for a better woman for me? Do you remember how you swore that I should not call you mother if I didn't leave Amy? Do you now say Amy is good for me?

1ST ELDER
What is this we are hearing, Afi? So you are directly behind all this mess?

MAN
And woman, why did you not allow your son to read the postmortem report? Don't you know that doctors spend time to do postmortem for a very good reason?

AFI
I didn't know then, but I know now.

2ND ELDER
The case is even more shameful than we thought. Afi, you never told us of your role in this predicament. You were a bad influence on your son.

AFI
But Teddy, I did it all for you. I could not bear to see your pain when you lost your two children. So when Nyamekye, the only surviving child, also became ill, I knew I had to act quickly. I had to get you a woman who could give you strong, healthy children.

TEDDY
So you did, Mother, and what happened? Where did that lead me? Oh, Mother, you have messed up my life. You have broken my home, scattered my family and brought me nothing but misery.

AFI
Believe me, Teddy my dear; it was never my intension to destroy your happiness. I wanted the best for you. I cared very much for you and your children. Please understand me.

AMY
Maa Afi, so it was you who made Teddy leave me? I took you as my own mother, loved and served you as any daughter should and that was my reward. You stabbed me in the back.

LAILA
And she is not satisfied with that. She has come again to stab you in the front too.

YABA
Leave Amy alone, Maa Afi, you will not get her this time. Look for a new wife for your son since you are an expert in that.

2ND ELDER
My brother, next time a woman invites us anywhere, let us be very careful, or she will lead us into trouble and embarrassment.

1ST ELDER
Especially when that woman happens to be Afi.

(Enter NIKKI, excited.)

NIKKI
Oh, Nyamekye, I am glad to see you well again. I said it. I said you would be well again.

(They rush into each other's arms.)

Look, I brought you this gift. My uncle brought it for me from the city, but I decided to give it to you. Here, take it. It is for you. My uncle said I can give it to you.

NYAMEKYE

Thank you very much, Nikki. You are the greatest friend in the whole wide world. And now that I am well again, we will work and play together as before. Come and stand by me as we get ready for church. You'll go with me, won't you? My mother and her friends are getting married in the church.

NIKKI

Sure, I will. And when we come back, I'll help you with all the lessons you missed when you fell ill.
(The adults look at the two children with admiration.)

MAA BEA

What a beautiful display of friendship, solidarity and love. We all need to cultivate the childlike spirit of faith, trust and devotion to make our world a better place.

AKU *(offstage)*

Nikki, Nikki, where are you? Oh, this boy will kill me. Come here, Nikki!
(Enters AKU, surprised and confused at the sight of the others.)

Oh… err… err… what's going on here?

NIKKI

Look, mother, Nyamekye is well again. I told you he will get better and right now I'm going with him to the church for his mother's wedding. Will you come along?

AKU

Maa Bea, please forgive me for not finding time to visit Nyamekye all this while he was ill. I am really sorry.

MAA BEA

But your son Nikki was here all the time to see Nyamekye, and I presumed he did so, on behalf of the family.

AKU

Yes... yes... you are right. Nikki represented all of us... the entire family. I'll rush home, put on my best cloth and join you. Yes, Nikki, my son, I'll be there. See you all soon.

(Exit AKU, hurriedly.)

2ND ELDER

Well, we must be going home now. Sorry for everything, Maa Bea.

MAA BEA

Actually, we were getting ready for the church to have our children's marriages blessed, when you came in. You are invited to join us in our happiness.

1ST ELDER

Well, I don't mind at all being part of anything that is honourable and enjoyable. I accept your invitation with all my heart.

2ND ELDER

Me, too. After our disgraceful mission I think I need something cheerful to brighten me up. I accept your kind invitation, Maa Bea.

AFI

Well, you two can stay and do whatever you like but certainly not I. Come, Teddy, let's go home.

TEDDY

No, mother, I am staying. I should have been firm long ago, but it's not too late.

AFI

Well, if that is what you want, Teddy, if it's your wish to stay here then I would stay and stand by you in case…

ELDERS

In case what… ? There is nothing you can do, Afi!

TEDDY

Yes Mother, we are staying. After the mess we've caused, the least we can do is to wish Amy and her friends all the best in their new stations. Thank you, Maa Bea. We gladly accept your invitation. And now Nyamekye, my son, I know I have not been the best of fathers to you, but I promise I shall never turn my back on you again, in sickness or in health. I've learnt my lesson. I know better now.

(Enter AKU, beautifully dressed and excited.)

AKU

I am here!

AYA and AWO

Right on time, Aku! You made it!

AKU

There is no way I'll miss this celebration. Amy and Nyamekye have fought and won a fierce fight, and we are all here to share in their well-deserved happiness and also thank God for His mercy upon us, His children.

DOLA

I must say we have all learnt a lot from what happened when the child fell ill.

KENNY

In fact, Amy my dear, your brave endurance, your remarkable fortitude and steadfast faith will be a perpetual source of inspiration to us.

DOLA *(to YABA and LAILA)*

And ladies, so will your unflinching support and incredible love for a friend in need.

AYEH

All these sterling qualities you displayed will guide us on our journey through life. And we in turn promise you love, happiness, prosperity and peace.

MAA BEA

Good words, good words, my children, and I hope you will all keep them. You must never run away from your responsibilities, no matter what or else you will unleash untold hardship on innocent people. Teddy, you can visit Nyamekye as often as you like, but he stays with his mother. And now it's time for us to get God's blessing for our children. Come on, we must get there before the officiating ministers. After that, we'll come home for merrymaking, feasting and more talking. Come, let's go to the church.

(Background music, "Here Comes the Bride." The couples led by NYAMEKYE and NIKKI, and all others in pairs move slowly and gracefully to the front to take their final bow.)

THE END

AFTERWORD

Long after we forgot all our lines and our cues to move to the center of the stage, we remembered the experience. We remembered the nerve-wracking moments when we waited patiently for the applause to invite us back on stage. We remembered the friendships forged through the many hours of rehearsals.

We quickly discovered that "When the Child Fell Ill" was a metaphor for life. Just when our young teenage minds would drift away from the invaluable meaning behind the play, Mrs. Charlotte Akyeampong would remind us of the significance of every word, and every line.
Maa Bea was the steady hand in Amy's otherwise tumultuous life. The other mother, Afi, was often shockingly shameful, but she painted well some of culture's odd expectations of women. Teddy became the central character whose decisions defined the arc of a family's life. Kenny imagined schemes, and had the good fortune to have Dola and Ayeh who didn't put up much of a resistance to any of his wild ideas. We fell in love with a story, and refined our passion for storytelling with Mrs. Akyeampong's unbridled love for art.
We took pride in memorizing the lines and song selections, just as we found it refreshing making stunning first impressions on audiences with whom we were fortunate to share the story. We saw teaching moments as we perceived the contrasts in the

characters, in their admirable grit and weakness.

One thing we knew was that even after the play ended, the scenes would replay in our minds over and again, and the lessons would impact us over and again. We would take our final bow and watch the curtains slowly fall, walk backstage and move on with our lives. The memories were soon to fade. But would they?

Once "When the Child Fell Ill" had been just a play, a life on a stage, waiting for an audience's applause in the end. It had been a journey to cherish and provided a jolt of laughter anytime a scene flashed in our mind. Many years later, the stage has turned out to be our own lives, without resetting, or rehearsals.

Occasionally, though, we hear the voice of Mrs. Akyeampong, shouting, "Cut, cut, please cut!"…"Well done, well done!"

The Cast and Crew, 1995

The play was first produced at PRESEC-LEGON and at the School of Performing Arts, University of Ghana, Legon in 1995 with the following cast:

THE CAST

MAA BEA	Adwoa Arnong
AMY	Barbara Ayesu
LAILA	Genevieve Kissi
YABA	Ama Serwah Acheampong
AWO	Yaa Biamah Ampadu-Sackey
AYA	Angela Adjei
NYAMEKYE	Kenneth Kanyagui
KENNY	Obeng-Amoako Edmonds
DOLA	Kwesi Ankomah
AYEH	Bruno Asafo
TEDDY	Lawrence Lawson
AFI	Kwarteokor Glover-Quartey
	Peace Ababio
	Frimpomaa Osei Tutu
1ST ELDER	David Doe
2ND ELDER	Ben Amissah-Ocran
	Castro Antwi Danso
MAN	Phillip Manu
DANCERS	Bernard Akoi-Jackson
	Donald Arko Gilbert
	Anthony Moses Prince Yankey
	BenEben Mfoafo McCarthy

THE CREW
DIRECTOR   Nii Lartey Awuletey
ASST. DIRECTOR/
CHOREOGRAPHER   Atta Owusu Xornam

PROPS
Living room furnishings
Towel
Purse containing money
Tray with jug of water and glasses
Bottle of schnapps with glass
Farming tools
Bottles of medication
Basket of fruit
Baskets of assorted foods and drinks
Two suitcases full of clothes
A tote bag

www.ingramcontent.com/pod-product-compliance
Lightning Source LLC
Chambersburg PA
CBHW020418080526
44584CB00014B/1388